LATITUDE

LATITUDE

Natasha Rao

The American Poetry Review
Philadelphia

For my family

Cover art by Georgina Taylor • Book design and composition: Gopa & Ted 2, Inc.

Distribution by Copper Canyon Press/Consortium

ISBN 978-0-9860938-4-5 (cloth, alk. paper) • ISBN 978-0-9860938-3-8 (pbk., alk. paper)

FIRST EDITION

We are asleep with compasses in our hands.
W. S. MERWIN

Longing, we say, because desire is full of
endless distances.
ROBERT HASS

Contents

Introduction

In troubled times, we see our traumatic revelations reflected in the poetry of the day. The world falls apart and so poetry mirrors the world and often falls apart, beautifully, tragically. Still, there is the search for a balance, and if not hope, some sort of resilience. After all, after winter, spring comes. Though we all may look different and deeply changed. But language, like the best grasses for weaving, bends and twists with the pressure that's applied. We rely on it to come with us, change with us, and somehow, if we are lucky, help us through to the other side.

The poems of Natasha Rao employ that bendable beauty of language. At once searching for a clarity and resisting a blunt narrative, Rao uses a language alive with imagination, surprising imagery, and a sense of unending longing for what has been lost. To be present in Rao's poetry is to witness the earth as an alive thing, each petal and fruit fly is paid attention to, there are no overly wrought, overly adorned lines that have forsaken the earth for the sake of poetry. Here, there is an honoring to both the human animal and the timelessness of the earth.

And time itself works differently in these poems. The past is woven through each poem like a recognizable color you can't quite name. There's a nostalgia that's not just explored, but interrogated, how the sheer idea of the past might allow someone to keep going. It's rare that I have read poems that argue with time in such a fierce manner. Time reverses or stands still or unravels or suddenly, in a sense of simultaneity; it is all happening at once. These are poems that honor not just the loss of time, but of what we took for granted, that moment before fear swallowed us all. The poet, in "For a Blue Page," writes with a painful clarity:

"Happiness is devastating
 in the past tense.

I lay these memories, like a fish,
on the cutting board."

This recognition of an almost overwhelming homesickness also speaks to the book's wrestling with the overarching theme of belonging. When our families are from a different country, when we are cleaved from our siblings, where do we find ourselves in the pulses of the world? In a triumphant long sequence in the center of the book, the poet unravels that sense of belonging and un-belonging with a series of prose poems that work as both vignettes of daily life and a study on shame and silence.

"Weekends I went to the park and said *aww* at passing dogs. Not knowing the names of breeds the way my white friends did, I sat in an embarrassed silence while they discussed their preferences for Dachshunds and Dobermans."

In the final section of that poem the speaker is passing through immigration and the reader sees that all that has come before is a recognition of not knowing exactly how to be in the world, how exactly to perform the self.

"Immigration. The counter, not the act. I cannot remember what expression to make, which of my faces appears in the passport photo. You see, sir, I am searching for relics. In degrees north to south. Childhood was a civilization that fell. I'm sorry, I don't know how to answer your question."

And if time and belonging are the main concerns of the book, there is also a recognition of complicity. What makes the speaker vulnerable, what she has taken for granted. The word "embarrassment" centers in two poems, and at a time where the speaker wishes she had spoken in the poem "What I Would Say," the poem instead ends with:

"Wanting to celebrate, we unearth the oldest bottle only to
discover
we waited too long and the cork has turned to clay. I would
like to
climb deep into the cellar of another life where I don't need
to be

drunk to tell my father how much I—"

Of course, in the great irony of poetry, we write what we wanted to say into a poem and our silence is then amplified into song. And these poems do that sort of singing. Singing in sorrow for an original innocence that is almost unbearable, but also singing the celebration of bearing witness to the passage of time.

In the sonic quality of the poems there is a sense of textured pleasure. Even in a poem like "Waking Days" where everything good has already happened, the sounds at the end of the poem let us inhale the details of the past like a longed-for delicacy.

"Look at her now in a room full of bankers, the way
she shrinks in the fluorescent light, dwelling in the past
tense, those long bright hours when she still felt
conviction to chase the shimmering fish,
still recognized herself in their certitude,
their obvious forward motion toward
some nameable goal."

There is a tenderness still for that shimmering fish. A tenderness for the family and the bridges both broken and being built between them. In that tenderness is a buoyancy that brings the reader into the present again and again. It is the work of these poems to acknowledge the lost things, but it is also the work of these poems to sharply point out the pleasure in the remembering.

Kay Ryan once wrote, "There must be a crack in the poet of some sort. It has to be deep, privately potent, and unmendable—and the poet must forever try to mend it." It is in that unmendable crack that these poems are made. Both attentive and quiet in their witnessing and brave and thunderous in their longing, Natasha Rao has made a book of poems that feels entirely, beautifully, human.

— Ada Limón, January 2021

I.

Old Growth

Backward crossovers into years before: airy
afternoons licking the wooden spoon, pouring soft blades
of grass from a shoe, all ways of saying I miss
my mother. I wish I could remember the gentle lilt
of my brother's early voice. Instead I hear clearly
the dripping of a basalt fountain. What gets saved—

My father fed my sick goldfish a frozen pea and it lived
for another six years. Outside, pears swathed in socks
ripened, protected from birds. Those bulbous
multicolored days, I felt safe before I knew
the word for it. But how to fossilize a feeling, sustain it
in amber? I keep dreaming in reverse until I reach
a quiet expanse of forest. The dragonflies are large
and prehistoric. Mother watches from a distance
as I move wildly, without fear.

Divine Transformation

Watching Jain nuns sweep peacock
feathers across the earth, I wanted to become
one of them. I was pupal, shifting
in the uniform of my larval skin. The nuns
practice ultimate nonviolence, brushing
the floor with fallen feathers, cotton broom,
unbleached wool to avoid bruising any insect.
It was to me an obvious way to live, before
I saw myself as small, inelastic. I was large
with guilt. Why girl, why not mouse, moth?
My mother asked where do you see your
self in ten years and I said barefoot, forest floor,
fostering compassion. Wearing a muslin cloth
over my mouth to avoid swallowing some
winged thing. I didn't auspicate the apartment
in Brooklyn, sponging blood from mosquitos
off my wall, could not imagine I would cultivate
a new cruelty, not just obvious roach spray
and rat trap, but killing the unobjectionable,
gnats and fruit flies who inhabit this arbitrary
world for just a breath. Last week I ate exclusively
the unborn, salmon roe and quail egg
in one luscious bite. The distance between
what I thought I was and what I am
grows. I could have been a kind of fly.
I could have been kind.

Fullness and Hunger

My father orders the crab *croquet*
and I am quick to correct
croquette for the white waiter
pouring water coquettishly.
Last summer in England I watched
my brother grip a mallet on the
manicured lawn of his new life
while my parents learned the rules
to this ballet, beaming, and I sipped
gin. My father's face when he
hit the ball through the wicket.
My father's face now. The slipped
grin. My father's face in my face.
I can be wicked, I begin to say, but
it sounds like crickets, it sounds
like nothing at all, though both
our mouths are moving.

What It Was Like

We had sushi that was so fresh we blushed.

Every seventeen years the cicadas rasped a kind of warning, showed us with increasing urgency the need to leave our old bodies behind.

I thought I could make some kind of difference. I thought I could memorize enough facts to stay composed in debates and not cry after one glass of wine when my brother says *we can all just go to Mars*.

I thought what I did was forgivable, in the grand scheme of things. That your love was an inexhaustible resource.

Terrible people made terrible decisions. Good people made terrible decisions. Which was I? It depended on the color of light in the bathroom, the angle at which I held my face to the mirror.

I lived in a city at sea level. See, levelheaded now, the frailty underfoot.

We pretended not to notice. We loved receiving shipments to our home, ceremoniously slashing packages with scissors, cleaving, leaving nothing but confetti.

It was like sitting across from you at dinner and wondering when to tell you. Knowing the worst is coming and simply ordering another drink.

Meanwhile the bubbles in the glass keep rising. It was luxurious. It was inevitable. It was a thick piece of fatty tuna, brimming with mercury, somehow effortless to swallow.

Radical Empathy

Because they shared bunk beds, eye shape, lilting
diction, read the same hardcover mythologies (she
the left page, he the right), the girl discovered she could be
her brother. One of them told a joke, the other delivered
the ending. In the grocery store she shouted
We switched brains! while her mother laughed, she really
believed it, felt she finally understood mathematics.
From the frozen aisle her brother said We switched back—
she hated the boundaries of her body then, almost knew
how it felt to live as a boy, loud in thick fabric.

She never grew out of the feeling that they were
interchangeable and thus capable of the same feats.
When he grew tall, took a date to prom, started working
at a bank, she tried the experiment. Closed her eyes to feel
the lapel, the purposeful gait. Instead there was only
her own mouselike silence, a graveyard of empty rooms.

Vulnerability Studies
after Solmaz Sharif

your floss in the trashcan
quiet, contorted

your fingers post orgasm
unbuckling the collar

your compliant signature
too embarrassed to dispute the bill

-

my father's google searches

his fumbling at the ticket machine,
serpentine line behind

his careful handwriting
on the graduation card: "i am sorry..."

-

lilies wearing only the desperate hum
of hornets looking for work

alone in the kitchen, lowering the pleated skirt
of a cupcake

something stuck to a shoe
a small wad of brain, freshly pink

Abecedarian on Shame

A mushroom quietly throbs with poison. I
bloat full of lies. Spurred by my
capacity for ruin, I insulted my brother
during the brief visit home, got too drunk in the
expensive restaurant while my mother's worry
fermented. When confronted with my lack of
gentleness, I blame birth control or the moon, but
haunted by the palpitations of a mouse stuck
in glue, I knew atonement was beyond my trapping.
Just months ago I shaved all my fur then
knelt naked in front of not-you, have
laid in unfamiliar beds, squeak becoming purr,
metamorphosing into whatever kind of
nocturnal creature strangers desire. I keep
offering the soft meat of myself to
people I meet on the internet, save the stinging
quills for those who love me. I don't know how to
reassemble myself into the kind of animal who
sniffs her way home every time. Somewhere,
there is a version of me whose instinct is to
tell the truth. She has no reason to
unravel in the doctor's office, no sudden fits of
viciousness and rage. She does the right thing even
when no one is looking. I envy her timeline, the
x-axis aligned. Somehow I grow more twisted, each
year eluding guilt with skill. It's easiest to pluck
zinnias if you don't look them in the face.

Crocus

First flower of spring pressing
through snow like plum trumpet,
proud young mouths awaiting rain.
A waxy and delicate promise
for earthworm month, sparrow season.
Last flower of winter pressing
through snow like end credits,
grand gesture, the urgent purpling
wound necessary for a warm
glossy blossoming that will follow.

Jasmine

Summer we rickshawed in silks,
milk shimmering in silver tins.
White garlands adorned gods on
plinths and mortals fragrant in
the kitchen. Clothesline August I
wore flowers in my hair,
history unbraided around me. I
learned lineage in the temple
and the sepal, family's long
threaded stems perfuming the air.

Daisy

No matter how often you
are called beautiful, it is
still possible to remain shy.
She removed her moonbeam robe
first. Then the dew dress.
Now in glaring light she
reveals the reserved purr of
yellow ochre in her throat.
She blushes while I stare
and quietly record my observations.

For a Blue Page

Tonight I am remembering
the Krishna-skin
skies of summer
& the way your laugh
made a Jacaranda tree bloom.
We slept in sheets the color of seaglass &
I woke with the taste of salt
in my mouth.
Happiness is devastating
in the past tense.
I lay these memories, like a fish,
on the cutting board.
Slice them open &
the deepest blue
spills onto this poem.

In my next life let me be a tomato

lusting and unafraid. In this bipedal incarnation
I have always been scared of my own ripening,
mother standing outside the fitting room door.
I only become bright after Bloody Mary's, only whole
in New Jersey summers where beefsteaks, like baubles,
sag in the yard, where we pass down heirlooms
in thin paper envelopes and I tend barefoot to a garden
that snakes with desire, unashamed to coil and spread.
Cherry Falls, Brandywine, Sweet Aperitif, I kneel
with a spool, staking and tying, checking each morning
after last night's thunderstorm only to find more
sprawl, the tomatoes have no fear of wind and water,
they gain power from the lightning, while I, in this version
of life, retreat in bed to wither. In this life, rabbits
are afraid of my clumsy gait. In the next, let them come
willingly to nibble my lowest limbs, my outstretched
arm always offering something sweet. I want to return
from reincarnation's spin covered in dirt and
buds. I want to be unabashed, audacious, to gobble
space, to blush deeper each day in the sun, knowing
I'll end up in an eager mouth. An overly ripe tomato
will begin sprouting, so excited it is for more life,
so intent to be part of this world, trellising wildly.
For every time in this life I have thought of dying, let me
yield that much fruit in my next, skeleton drooping
under the weight of my own vivacity as I spread to take
more of this air, this fencepost, this forgiving light.

II.

In the New Year

Sun on my face and the train slips

      into the tunnel. Dim reflection confronts.

Perhaps I am lacking in something substantial

      like iron, or virtue. How easy it is to hurt

someone, how hard to face what comes after.

      My face, strangely lit, in the bathroom

mirror. Surrounded by friends, I felt a queasy

      aloneness, didn't know whose lap to cry into.

Someone spat out an olive pit. Someone tore

      streamers off the wall. I distorted

through the stemmed glass. Already exhausted

      in this angular year, where I hover

like a stranger to my own life.

      No resolution in any of it.

For a Gray Page

achromatic exhale
thinned glossy
then wet.

when I see Van Eyck's
gray angels, I want
to pleat myself

into stone. grisaille,
the private under-
painting, secret I know

to be true. the real me
a naked mono-
chrome layer of oil.

a monk dons his gray robe
of humility the same instant
I unhook my bra

for the portrait.
my mouth all ash,
memory gravel.

a mouse, an elephant, a black-
out all swim in the gray
matter of my mind,

so often, these days,
rendered glasslike. I would
like, for a moment,

to be vapor,
inkwash, a hailstone
melting unnoticed.

Warm Enough

I kissed a friend on the mouth
first on a beach

then in a dream. In life
there was a stray dog
cows inside a low fence
curls crisp with salt

In the dream we were older
it somehow changed me

I woke and remembered breaking
the exoskeleton of shrimp
those round eyes
my beautiful friend

Both kisses equally un
real. Unbraiding my hair
somewhere sunny

Which version held the milk
of coconuts? My mind is a sieve
on the shore, his mouth

no, my mouth the only certainty
my longing
an empty shell

Intimacy Fair

The initial intimacy:
Waking to parallelograms
of light

A quivering intimacy:
A leaf, outreached
to save the gleaming beetle
from drowning in the pool

The intimacy of the crowd:
Running across the platform
from local to express

Teenage intimacy:
Sharing half the bottle
then half the gum
after vomiting

Drenched intimacies:
Wrists of rain
extending from an umbrella

Shouldering
stalks of sunflowers
during the storm

Bunk bed intimacy:
The moon wrapping us
in white blankets

Listening to apples
fall in the grass outside

Gleaming intimacy:
The shock of silver
on the back molars
of a familiar mouth opened wide

A blurred intimacy:
Your forehead after
a broken fever

A slippery intimacy:
Swallowing baby squid
checking each other's tongues
for ink

Ultimate intimacy:
Moments wholly
for ourselves

Catching sight of my face
alone in the rearview mirror

Feeling for the ripeness
of plums

Sighing upward
then wiping birdshit from my hair

For My Brother

The backseat of dad's
car, warm limbs
pressing, stale sleep
smell in our mouths.
Whenever heads touched,
our dreams were related
by blood. It all was a kind
of magic, then. Now
I get off the plane
and keep waiting for the part
where you need me again.
We eat Turkish delight
wrapped in tissue paper,
and the gaunt moon
salivates. Years ago
we stood side by side
on the driveway at night,
moths spilling white dust
onto our palms.

My Father's First Night in the National Defense Academy

In these barracks, night speaks another dialect.
No longer does he fall asleep to the smell
of boiling milk or his brother breathing
cigarettes in the dark. He doesn't yet know
the ways his body will change for a war
that doesn't happen in this country
he will soon leave. From now on he will grow
like sharpening. Tonight he is too eager and
cannot sleep, this last moment before they strip him
of childhood, have him believe the true war
is inside him. Tonight, he is still a boy of sixteen
who dreams of being a pilot, not to fight
but to soar, titanium wings fluttering
through the blameless air. He brushes the blanket,
this fleshy creature with no edges, not yet bruised
into the solemn duty of manhood.

My Mother's First Summer Away from Home

On top of a bullock cart is a bale of hay
atop the hay is a small brown suitcase
and next to the suitcase is my mother. She is six.

She will spend the summer shooing crows
from sundried pickles and learning English
grammar from encyclopedias on a tall shelf.

The shelf is my great grandfather's. We will
never meet, and I will not be able to imagine
his face. My mother had a boldfaced childhood

laughing in languages I don't speak. I am jealous
of the clerk who sold her rubber balls, the priest
spooning Prasad into her small palm, the insects

watching through glass as she moves freely,
unbugged by obligation. My mother and I
are stuck in an asymmetrical embrace.

I want to know her as she knows me, full
of love from the first word. At six,
she memorized tenses in books, the way

I spend days with sun-stained fragments,
thinking I might be able to learn
everything, afraid to miss any small part.

World View

Envious of the fly
that has enough eyes
to take everything in
and the snake
who can swallow it
whole.

Love Letters
at the Scripps National Spelling Bee

To know the shape of every word, to guide graphemes' glottal slide,
to fold yourself inside arch and bowl, to feel your body brush, like
a B-O-U-G-A-I-N-V-I-L-L-E-A's vine, against every line, to claim
language as your own, to step onstage and pull a book out of your mind.
The camera pans to parents' clasped hands and suddenly I am six,
C-Y-M-O-T-R-I-C-H-O-U-S and transfixed as my father teaches me
to play chess. He lists grandmasters and says with an air
of P-R-O-S-P-I-C-I-E-N-C-E, that could be you some day. I picture
myself atop a giant rook, long black hair trellising down the side.
When the shape of my ambition becomes writing, I notice names in each
F-E-U-I-L-L-E-T-O-N are the same, all Smith and Jones and Miller. Still
my parents are devoted to my detailed desire. At school I say Rao
is pronounced like wow, then smile. On TV at the Bee I see Anisha (wow),
Rohan (wow), Srinidhi (wow) as though they are an extension of myself,
we are S-C-H-E-R-E-N-S-C-H-N-I-T-T-E figures linking hands. From now
on this is how I see community, one rectangular arm flowing wordlessly
into the next. At the Community Park my brother and I spread scraps
of bread, piqued by ducks' beaks and their otherworldly P-A-L-A-M-A. All week
my vegetarian mother wakes early to assemble our turkey sandwiches
with mayonnaise, cuts off the crust. We offer no G-U-E-R-D-O-N. We bring
trimmed bread ends to the pond, entertained by manic bleating and webbed
feet. I can't help but watch swans in the periphery, something familiar
in beautiful creatures unaware that I exist. Onstage, I can't gauge
between floating and frantic paddling. How I admire their confident tread!
I become P-O-C-U-R-A-N-T-E during conversations about an athlete's score,
excuse myself to sit in the bathroom, the C-H-I-A-R-O-S-C-U-R-I-C quiet
of a chessboard floor. But I could talk all night about my heroes at the Bee,
never L-A-O-D-I-C-E-A-N, (I wish it were me), the way they have taken
their goal to completion. The announcers say they dominated, they killed,
they have mastered the dictionary, like men with A-I-G-U-I-L-L-E-T-T-Es
who weaponized this language before, but here there are no stingers, only
children's voices like honey bubbling through prismatic wax. How can anyone
say you don't belong in a country if at twelve you have already swum through

its alphabet, catching crumbs along the way, have stalemated orthography itself. The parents are crying and I am crying and pride is quantifiable, you can use it in a sentence, you can use it your whole life. Even the swans are applauding.

Note: All capitalized words are winning words from past Scripps National Spelling Bees

Earth Memory

I.   Goose foot. Geese feet. Daffodils in mason jars. Once, I watched a fruit fly drown in my vodka and orange juice. I write on my wrist: a lake is a good place to contemplate the past. Erase the last word with saliva and instead, write: future. It's spring, but I'm cold. All I ever wanted was someone to read my goosebumps like Braille.

II.   I walk the path where we caught frogs in Tupperware containers and used hand sanitizer before eating sandwiches on the bench. The same river is still here. Same muggy morning, same algae skin slowly peeling from it, same sky sliding downstream. This is the way things were/are/will be. Probably.

III.   Once in an air-conditioned lecture hall, my biology professor told us that goosebumps are a vestigial structure. I thought about the ghosts of chimpanzees. The professor kept talking but I wanted to stand up and yell Stop! Wait! Tell us more, please, about the ghosts in our skin, tell us about our history and how we have been recycled! Instead, kept tracing my thigh in silence.

Chorus

A cul-de-sac of televisions
switched to the same channel.
Overhead, the bleating of geese.
Attention, these days, is held
for a brief moment, the way
I might hold onions
at the market. I watch the stock
simmer on the stove. I gather,
refresh, then trade
the screen for the window,
where snow is falling decisively
in the same direction. Look
away, look back, it's already done.
I fling wide the door to feel
which way the wind is moving,
barely open my mouth before
a new species of bird evolves
and fills the air
with uncountable versions
of the freshest song.

Novembering

wet leaves and the deer that eat them

milkweed pods

wild, untrimmed light

-

rotting pulpous pears

mushrooms in maple shadow

-

a day is like any other until you remember
what other days are like

-

freckled feathers

bats beneath a slate roof

the slick throbbing worm

-

silly me
i am singing of beauty again

under burning rain
in the poisoned forest
i can't help but open my deciduous mouth

Decembering

This city disintegrates into fat flakes and spills
a billowing silence over crooked branches
of birch, bowtied bags, an ambulance. The grid
exhales. Times Square in dress rehearsal
practices its celebration for a new decade knee
deep in confetti. The countdown could be
for a departed era, the way snow trembles around
brass lamps, wind unbraiding a woman's hair.
The city is a forest, a village, an empty cathedral.
It is almost impossible to believe in the yellow-
lit tunnels of trumpets beneath my feet,
a damp and relentless scurrying. New York
is layered with dens. Roofs keep hidden
the secret of bats, their dark bickering elbows,
and below the sink, mice take precise bites
of white bread. In my own nest I spread a buttery
light and drink red wine assiduously. I desire
velvet and lace, oysters in June but pearls
in December, silk, warm milk, the low notes
of a bassoon through the window before
my thick, ursine sleep. I will wake only in time
for flakes to become white butterflies feasting
on the first fleecy buds while I fix my fur,
hungry once more to see the city reflected
in your eyes, those dark, glimmering berries.

Light Years

These days everyone is moving away, folding flaps of the past
into boxes. If the house goes, I think, so, too, does the feeling.
Each time it is the same, a few martinis in the city and I dream
of clementines huddled inside the net. Black-eyed Susans
and all those trails unwalked. In the bathroom I swallow
or snort that loaded syllable *home*. My tired teeth in the mirror.

My brother lives in another country. My parents left
the country in which they were born. Somehow I am tethered
to this place, the fading grass, all the left turns I built up
the courage to make. No—most days I wake and ache
to leave this continent, this time, this body. I stay from fear.
Those were the lightest years. If I go, so, too, does the feeling.

III.

Latitude

I.

Back then I was committed to the color blue, felt moved to paint my walls. nails, furniture the same shade of teal. Now my body swells at the window with casual longing. Do you believe in saltwater gargling. As a cure. At the gas station I felt proud to specify it was the navy lighter we wanted. Often the bravest thing I do all day is open my mouth. On every beach washes up the memory of some other beach when I didn't evaluate my own body. Last night Orion's Belt filled me with dread because everyone I have shown it to has exited my life with no warning. Still, I couldn't help myself. The light was brief and obvious.

II.

In the liquor store I remembered a friend's advancements with unexpected enjoyment. To feel desired. The precedent to shame. Being alone in a new, warm place fills me with recklessness that I have never tried to quell. I watch my skin darken in the sun before putting on a white dress. I am looking for affirmation, something glittering and encrusted with shape. How to explain, even to oneself. Truthfully I didn't mind the smell of semen in the air. The bartender speared blackberries on a toothpick over and over. The hotel parrot had the voice of a lonely child.

III.

Weekends I went to the park and said *aww* at passing dogs.
Not knowing the names of breeds the way my white friends
did, I sat in an embarrassed silence while they discussed
their preferences for Dachshunds and Dobermans. I knew
the names of plants and trees and constellations but kept
this to myself, could never sit in a white circle and change
the color of conversation. What I liked was sitting in the
passenger seat while a capable person found a place to
pull over. The hyperbolic shooting stars. I marveled at
heaven and the person and felt lucky I had found them,
their unabashed turn signals and disregard for trespassing
signs. I was light and fearless by proxy. The next morning
we drove further into the park and, like a small, round peb-
ble, a noise slipped from my mouth when I saw the geyser
surge. The same mineraled gasp the first time I felt a man
erupt inside me. All that giddy bubbling. Grand prismatic.
Oh. It's so unearthly here on earth.

IV.

Whitefish and red wine. Again, the barking of stray dogs.
Something unpronounceable at the back of my throat. I
followed my friend into her new life, drove through tunnel
after tunnel in Italy, undressed and jumped into the lake.
As soon as I remembered I could be anyone I took off my
silly costume and let out a limoncellolaugh. Ate a nectar-
ine on the dock. *Beauty is the answer*, I thought simply, but
before I knew to what, I transformed back into myself and,
towel-less, began to shiver.

V.

Newly blueberried air. A man said *percolating* underneath
the full moon and walked me to my car with a calculable
expression. To stand in front of the brook in total darkness.
To be convinced of something you can't see. While he tried
unsuccessfully to open the bottle of wine, I felt tenderness
but disappointment, a sadness for us both, the inevitabil-
ity of after the affair when we slip back into our ingrained
lives. I motioned for the corkscrew. He mentioned God. I
was surprised, given the scandalous nature of the evening,
how predictable it all was. Except for the wet grass in the
meadow which was, somehow, unimaginable.

VI.

In Spain, my brother and I side by side in twin beds awoke
the same moment beneath a squid ink sky. We had both
been dreaming of soup. Outside, feral cats slunk in and out
of ancient ruins. A day is like any other until you remem-
ber what other days are like. In the plaza so many hands
were moving, everyone had something to say, the birds,
the fountain, the small dishes groaning with sauce, and I
felt unbearably embarrassed for my own silence, the blank
desertion of my unreliable voice.

VII.

The whole day through yellow tinted glasses. Nearby, a
fish is being fried. A pilot pulls the yoke. Two girls crest the
wave. I spend all night with friends on the deck, a semicircle
of wet bathing suits. Once before I sat like this under stars,
cross-legged, but the world was so small then. I lived in the
horse pen, ate sugar and apples. This week I am unable to
contribute to conversation, determined to hear every voice
at once. All half nods, my ears agape. Somewhere on the
island, a dog howls in pain. A trawl net drags ominously. I
unwish, I take it back, I don't want to be a fly, to know every-
thing happening at once. As it is, I can't go a day without
breaking my own buzzing heart.

VIII.

To cut all ties. To not know what comes next. To watch
my nails grow longer, having forgotten to pack the clip-
per. After being admonished by the flight attendant I felt
small, eating my ice cream with a thin wooden spoon. I
thought maybe if I lived in that place or wore that kind
of skirt, those earrings, I would have a life without regret.
What a relief, at last, to admit I am in love with turbu-
lence. To be flung through the air at immeasurable speed.
To glare into the blue gelatin ocean, the dissolving past.

IX.

Bonfire Night. The crags of Arthur's Seat. Months before, I watched my mother pray at the foot of her bed, knowing it was for me. Hazelnut wafers. A thin, oily, gravy ladled onto my plate. What I loved most was the color of the city. No, what I loved most was the person I could be. In her letter my friend described: *a happiness unsurprising and as expected as air, not a frightening burst of euphoria that will leave you dull and still after it is gone.* Steeple and stone. A soft amplitude of rain. In this version of reincarnation I can remember all my lives.

X.

Immigration. The counter, not the act. I cannot determine what expression to make, which of my faces appears in the passport photo. You see, sir, I am searching for relics. In degrees north to south. Childhood was a civilization that fell. I'm sorry I don't know how to answer your question.

IV.

Type to Learn

In fourth grade
they put our hands
under shoe boxes
to see how fast
we could say:
fox moves quickly I
am Sam but really
the words they
should have prepared
us to type fast
with our eyes
closed were time
is running out things
are terribly wrong
and I miss you
so much. The world
is different now
or what's different
is that I know
of its dangers
this week on TV
another long-awaited
trial the verdict again
unjust I cried then typed
one long sentence
I'm still a small body
on a big planet I'm still
the same person thinking
about foxes and the speed
at which they can run
and I wonder if
Mrs. Cannatelli knew
which animals
would disappear first
I guess there's a lot

I didn't see coming
I remember not being
afraid I remember
eraser caps and having
the highest typing score
and that being all
that mattered
as though perfection
were a guarantee
of survival as though
with enough practice
I would be equipped
for any of this.

The Truth

I am only kind to my father
in poems he will never read.

I try to imagine him small
the way my grandmother tells it:

patient, deerlimbed, pondering
polynomials. Wanting only

a Toblerone bar for his birthday
to eat alone in his room

away from the violence of exploding
raindrops, pitiless Madras summer.

I wonder if he is proud
of his life like I am proud

of my poems—the best
we could do. In another world

I would go down the stairs
to where my father is sitting alone

with his wine glass and I would tell him
I'm sorry. But I am a woman

the same way my father is a man: always
a little embarrassed.

Somehow it is easier to say I hated
practicing piano in the morning

than it is to say I loved
the way you turned the pages for me.

I cringed being woken up each morning,
pulled blinds and tough light, but I loved

your warm and capable hands on my forehead
brushing away the remnants of a dream.

River Road

Returning from the airport I felt a sadness I thought
I couldn't survive. The old motions sliced in half.
You no longer in the busy parking lot to quell to

laugh when I say what the fuck which way how do I
and it sounds frightening coming out of my mouth
in an empty car. My voice an unpaved road. We spent

the whole summer driving, lucid dreaming with music
and colors in slow blur. Alone I do everything
with nervous as prefix, but with you I took those bends

blissfully. So many years living beside the twisting road
and we never got used to the word *roadkill*,
the flippancy of it. You grab my arm at the unfurled

intestine and just like that I become the big sister
again, rolling up the windows and maneuvering
the curves. It's okay. You can look now. Look—

your existence was the best thing that happened
to me. Come back across the phone, the ocean
come back across the hall where I am growing old

waiting for you, pass me the keys and we will feel
alive again. In the almost-world where you sit shotgun,
the deer still has its spots. We saw it coming.

Haystacks

Effect of Snow and Sun, Monet (1891)

> Evening is wearing a dress
> the color of amethyst. Shadows
> tug at the hem.

at Sunset near Giverny, Monet (1891)

> A wounded sun begins to bleed.
> Bales of hay absorb coppery
> syrup that spills in drops.

Snow Effect, Monet (1891)

> The countryside holds its breath,
> expectant. Birds pause mid-song.
> They exhale only once snow falls
> like sifted flour on the bowled world.

* * *

The Impressionists painted moments they knew would disappear.
You are sleeping. Grains gathering in the corners of your eyes.

For a Yellow Page

numinous rain
and the grid softens

edges feel less
like edges

we shoo the starling
from the sparrow's nest

the kitchen smells
of lemon tart

in earthworm month
daffodil colored afternoon—

buds smooth with fur,
tulips,

your mouth tender
and urgent as new grass

Confessional Poem

Despite my efforts to remain indifferent, I hate that my boyfriend has dated girls with names I use all the time, like Summer and May. I hate that they have all been blonde, that they look like summer and May. Petalsoft, pink. I say *I can't believe April is over* and *Finally, the warmest season,* not wanting to remind him of their soft charms. Not wanting, myself, to imagine Summer's breezy laugh or May's gentle body unfurling around him.

The first time I had sex with someone white, I felt he was staring into the darkest parts of me, so I did all kinds of things to make him close his eyes. I want to ask my boyfriend if it was like that for him, with Summer after prom, if he felt his brown body darken next to hers like fruit in the sun.

But I know the answer. One night, thoughtlessly drunk on self-doubt and rum, I opened his journal. Oh, how he loved those blossomy girls. It was only when I saw my own name in careful handwriting that I shut the book and cried.

I confess: I am selfish. I just want to know that someday, if this world ends, there will never exist another in which your familiar mouth forgets the feel of my name.

OR

Forgive earthworms
for contorting. Prioritize
forests before work
or glory. Worship dormice.
Forsake ordinariness,
forget conformity, gorge words
euphorically—stories immortalize
orgasm, horseflies, floral
histories. Workshop emperors
or gladiators rigorously.
Explore discomfort, remorseless
scorpions or forbidden
seafloors. Reforest, dechlorinate,
evaporate fluorescents.
Memorize aphorisms
before performing
thunderstorms unforgettably.
Endeavor for gorgeous,
borderless worlds, multicolored
unanchored orchestras.
Orbit memorably.

Another Spring

Another failed chance to vault froglike
into a new life. It's pre-green, thinned
acrylic approximating watercolor,
and with a paintbrush I am pollinating
lemon trees, impersonating bees. Still
so far from honeyed. I couldn't kill
a stinkbug, but somehow it was easy
to betray you. Ants swarmed
the semen-damp cloth. Releasing
their glossy bodies into moss,
I allowed myself to pretend
I am not monstrous. Every year
this ritual. Spring is only a performance
of reinvention, the flowers keep becoming
themselves. Always the stinkbug concealed
behind its shield, the hungry, horny ants,
the sparrow undoing her nest as I
pull apart my life. I have to believe
azalea buds might swoon into forsythia
while nearby snow melts to milk. Some proof
I could become improbably gentle, good
as drops of water on turned dirt.

Waking Days

In childhood she was magnificent, or she believed

herself to be. The deck was hedged with marigolds.

Tomatoes dangled boldly in the yard. At

four she spelled *cornucopia* for delighted adults,

not her first instance of pride, but the first

she would be able to remember. Hers was a youth

of ambition, round, ripe days overflowing

from a goat's horn. If she felt lonely, it was only

because the color of blackberry juice made her swell

on the cusp of something unbearably profound,

for which she had no words. Gradually

she understood neither the world nor herself

were what she had imagined. Became a small

fleshy thing in a honking, angular place. Once,

sobering up in a hospital gown, she almost

recalled that nameless awe, so close

was her stain's resemblance to that of some dark

fruit. So slippery her sense of being alive.

She learned how to make the city feel

like moving underwater, how to hold her breath.

Look at her now, in a room full of bankers, the way

she shrinks in fluorescent light, dwelling in the past

tense, those long bright hours when she still felt

conviction to chase the shimmering fish,

still recognized herself in their certitude,

their obvious forward motion toward

some nameable goal.

Small Pond

We were softly enormous. Hooked on
lengthening light, healthy calves pedaling
to the trailhead. We knew everyone
in every grocery store. We knew the code
to the high school tennis shed. We learned
language for the world around us, dogwood,
larkspur, pointed to ants and said head,
thorax, abdomen, back when we imagined
the world narrow enough to name.
Squatting above our reflections, we filled
Ziploc bags with minnows, never
considered the ways a body might change
in its container. Last week in Brooklyn,
coming down or hungover, I floated
through the park with a friend. Magnolia
he said. I put my left foot in front of my right.
Gingko. Think of all the directions a life
can take. It's true I love spooning pâté
and telling white lies, spinning while the first birds
blow their trumpets and the budding
world feels like mine again. I want wildness
anywhere I can find it, in flowerless hours, the city
a thicket of unnamable parts. I return to my corner
of girlhood shrunken, shocked by the crabapple's
pink and the unapologetic dandelions, the way
they remind me of yesterday's concentric world.
Throw a rock and the water will ripple further
from where it started, each ring bewildered
by the shape that came before.

My Brother Is Accused of Making a Bomb
but Admits He Was Just Trying to Get High

Across the ocean my brother unscrews
a flask of ether. The dark hits early
in November. He tells me he is bored, his
mind explosive. We recount our old
topography, the time we stole mushrooms
from the lapel of a long afternoon.

Chemical or not, something has changed.
Sometimes I miss my brother so much
I force-feed myself last night's dream.
Board the plane and pray to recognize
the person who will greet me. The familiar
burst, like the color orange in my stomach.

As children we mixed lemon juice and water
to make invisible ink and wrote glistening
secret letters. I am startled by how much
I still need him to hold my words
above the flame and understand
what I am unable to say to anyone else.

What I Would Say

I'm sorry. My father spent two hundred dollars on ice skates that sleep under a blanket of dust. Also, a violin. Also, a saddle. I complained about the heat at the Colosseum. Also, at the Taj Mahal. I had pink eye at the Leaning Tower of Pisa and frowned in all the photos, wearing my brother's sunglasses.

Staring at my face, strangely lit, in a changing room mirror. I want to be like him, I am scared I am becoming him, I am not sure if my nose is my own.

Wanting to celebrate, we unearth the oldest bottle only to discover we waited too long and the cork has turned to clay. I would like to climb deep into the cellar of another life where I don't need to be drunk to tell my father how much I—

Diwali

My whole life
has been a festival
of light. Window seats
open blinds sun
syrup in a jar
with breakfast. Cold
blooded girl like
naked lizard on velvet
couch, waiting for muscles
to heat, become limber.
Everything feels
otherworldly
soaked in light, palms
lightly soaked. Yellow
ochre in the throat
Slick wicks, small flame
in clay, bouquet
of burning oil. Shouting
with delight beneath
fireworks, bodies vibrating
like guitar strings plucked
to life—I have never
been any good at prayer
or worship, but my
God,
I believe in celebration.

Witness

I lived on top of the roof, staring at the Jehovah's Witness
turrets. I lived making up metaphors about the moon

while Bobby balanced a boombox above his shoulders
and squirrels shyly swallowed the spiked heads

of passionflowers, pilfering grape tomatoes and averting
my gaze. I watched the other girls and made notes of

how to be more like that, how to wear a shirt that hangs off
the left shoulder, how to align my body with everything

I've ever wanted. I loved when, at the wine store,
it turned out they already had my name in the system.

It's true there are so many versions of a self,
sometimes one forgets how to walk like the other.

In swimmy reflections or in glasses clean, I watched myself
enjoy being seen, witnessed my evolution into

loud-laughing, cross-legged, can you play the song that
reminds us all where we have been? Inside me is a girl opening

a red locker, unable to envision so many glistening eyes
listening when she opens her mouth. Here I am

with my hair up, socked foot on your leg. Falling
in love again. Let's toast to pizza. Let's order the moon!

With you at last I climb down from my watchtower
and step into the whitelit present tense.

Late August

Autumn oversleeps. Stale
summer breeze slips
through the kitchen window
in this city that's never heard
your laughter. *See you soon*
I said, then I never
saw you again. I am trying
to suck on this impossible
world as if it were a piece
of ice in my mouth.
Outside, an orange robin
is laying blue eggs.

Coney Island

The Q train empty enough for vodka
lemonades, lurching through a morning
we can see out the window. O Luna Park,
mustard arcana, dystopic soap opera
in circus stripes!

In photos, our faces are panicked, though
we insist we are roundmouthed with joy.
Beneath the aquarium tunnel we kiss
with the urgency of those who know
what is about to happen. We eat clams
on the half shell, drink tequila in the dark,
have sex on the disreputable Ferris wheel.

Ours is the euphoria of finality. Here—
the last oyster on earth, dolloped with
mignonette. The last turnstile click
before the neon ballad expires. We bask
in the shrieks of the gloriously alive
beachgoers, thrill-seekers, foam moles
evading the mallet.

Ritual

The flowers of my childhood
are not the flowers of my mother's
childhood, but it is easy to mistake
forsythia for gorse. After dinner,
I clear the plates and my father
offers fennel seeds in a jar. This
is how we live year after year,
auspicious and barefoot in a temple
of trees we did not plant.

Acknowledgments

Thank you to the editors of the following publications, in which some of the poems in this collection first appeared:

The Adroit Journal: "In My Next Life Let Me Be a Tomato" and "Another Spring"

The American Poetry Review: "What It Was Like"

Bennington Review: "Type to Learn"

The Los Angeles Review of Books Quarterly Journal: "Chorus"

The Margins: "Latitude I"

Narrative: "Old Growth" and "The Truth"

The Nation: "In the New Year"

The Offing: "For my Brother"

Palette Poetry: "Abecedarian on Shame"

Poetry Northwest: "For a Gray Page"

Rattle: "For a Blue Page"

Yale Review: "Divine Transformation" and "Fullness and Hunger"

A million thanks to Ada Limón for selecting this manuscript. I can't read your introduction without crying the most incredulous tears, and I am so grateful. Thanks, too, for all of your poems, which have quite literally changed my life.

My deepest, heartfelt thanks to each of my teachers from grade school to graduate school, without whom this collection would not exist. I am especially indebted to: Catherine Barnett, Deborah Landau, Meghan O'Rourke, Matthew Rohrer, Sharon Olds, Terrance Hayes, Ed Hirsch, Rick Benjamin, Gale Nelson, Sally Wen Mao, Liz Cutler, Judy Michaels, Karen Latham, and Barbara Walker. Your support over the years has been my guiding light, and I feel like the luckiest person in the world to have learned from all of you.

I also have endless gratitude for my MFA cohort at NYU, who redefined for me what a poem can be, and who made me feel like a Real Life Poet over karaoke and glasses of wine. Thank you for your wisdom and close reading: Kyle Lopez, Wo Chan, Hannah Hirsh,

Will Frazier, Sarina Romero, Jiaoyang Li, Gbenga Adesina, Chloe Blog, Karisma Price, India Gonzalez, Sasha Debevec-McKenney, Bernard Ferguson, Ben Zaidi, and Sonja Bjelic. Thanks also to my entire Bread Loaf family, and especially my sister and lifelong first reader, Stephanie Wobby. I love you and can't thank you enough for your encouragement and decision-making, not just for this book, but in all things. Thanks also to Taneum Bambrick for being the most generous, brilliant inspiration, in whose footsteps I am so honored to follow.

Many thanks to the Creative Writing Program at NYU, the Bread Loaf Writers' Conference, and the Literary Arts department at Brown University. Thank you to the Honickman Foundation, The American Poetry Review, and Copper Canyon. And a thunderous standing ovation to Elizabeth Scanlon for your guidance and care, it has been a true delight to work with you.

t wouldn't be an acknowledgements section without me tearing up over my dear friends—for your encouragement, for facilitating several of the situations that became poems in this book, and for being essential sources of joy. Thank you Jonathan Gibbons for your many years of love and belief, and for being my reader since the blue backpack days. Caitlyn Matchick, Tomas Navia, Jeffrey Gibbons, Diego Arene-Morley, Maya Code-Williams, Marissa Traina, Prescott Smith, Bobby Klapper, Andrew Little, Christiano Boria, Liam Trotzuk, Alexa Wybraniec, Adriana van Manen, Yvonne Cha, Kenny Lusk, Caroline Orr, Ben Shack-Sackler, Ted Clifford, Lily Halpern, I love you all, and every day with you is a poem. I really couldn't have done it without you Rakesh, thank you for your patience and your extraordinary heart.

And of course, thank you to my loving family for everything. To my parents, grandparents, and Navin: each word I write is for you. You are the very best part of my world.

Notes

"What It Was Like" was written in the immediate afterglow of reading Brenda Shaughnessy's *The Octopus Museum*

"Radical Empathy" was inspired by Zbigniew Herbert's "Sister"

"Vulnerability Studies" is in direct response to Solmaz Sharif's "Vulnerability Study"

The title "For a Blue Page" was given to me as a prompt by my professor and wonderful poet Gale Nelson

"Intimacy Fair" takes its structure from Wisława Szymborska's "Miracle Fair"

"Love Letters" was written after watching the documentary *Spelling the Dream*

"Earth Memory" is a response to Bhanu Kapil's fascinating question from *The Vertical Interrogation of Strangers*, "What do you remember about the earth?"

In "Latitude IX," the friend whose letter I've quoted is Adriana van Manen, whose words have sustained me in any and every city (I only wish that I could convey her looping handwriting here, too)

"OR" was inspired by Nicole Sealey's exquisite poem "And"

www.ingramcontent.com/pod-product-compliance
Lightning Source LLC
Chambersburg PA
CBHW030855090426
42737CB00009B/1234